Bumble Bees

by Cheryl Coughlan

Consulting Editor: Gail Saunders-Smith, Ph.D.

Consultant: Gary A. Dunn, Director of Education,
Young Entomologists' Society

Pebble Books

an imprint of Capstone Press
Mankato, Minnesota

1

Pebble Books are published by Capstone Press
818 North Willow Street, Mankato, Minnesota 56001
http://www.capstone-press.com

Library of Congress Cataloging-in-Publication Data
Coughlan, Cheryl.
    Bumble bees/by Cheryl Coughlan.
    p. cm.—(Insects)
    Includes bibliographical references (p. 23) and index.
    Summary: Simple text and photographs present the color and body parts
of bumblebees.
    ISBN 0-7368-0236-3
    1. Bumblebees—Juvenile literature. [1. Bumblebees.] I. Title. II. Series: Insects
(Mankato, Minn.)
QL568.A6C589   1999
595.79′9—dc21

                                                                98-49431
                                                                     CIP
                                                                     AC

Note to Parents and Teachers

The Insects series supports national science standards for units on
the diversity and unity of life. The series shows that animals have
features that help them live in different environments. This book
describes and illustrates the parts of bumble bees. The photographs
support early readers in understanding the text. The repetition of
words and phrases helps early readers learn new words. This book
also introduces early readers to subject-specific vocabulary words,
which are defined in the Words to Know section. Early readers may
need assistance to read some words and to use the Table of
Contents, Words to Know, Read More, Internet Sites, and
Index/Word List sections of the book.

Table of Contents

4

Most bumble bees are black and yellow.

6

Bumble bees are
big and hairy.

antennas

Bumble bees have
two antennas.

eyes

Bumble bees have
two large eyes.

Bumble bees have
three small eyes.

tongue

Bumble bees have
a long tongue.

Bumble bees use their tongue to drink nectar.

Bumble bees have
four thin wings.

Bumble bees buzz
when they fly.

Words to Know

antenna—a feeler on an insect's head; bumble bees feel and smell with antennas.

eye—a body part used for seeing; bumble bees have two large, compound eyes made of many small lenses; bumble bees' three small eyes detect light and dark.

nectar—a sweet liquid bumble bees gather from flowers

tongue—a mouthpart bees use to drink water and nectar; the tongue and other mouthparts come together to form a proboscis.

wing—a movable part of an insect that helps it fly

Read More

Crewe, Sabrina. *The Bee.* Life Cycles. Austin, Texas: Raintree Steck-Vaughn, 1997.

Fowler, Allan. *Busy, Buzzy Bees.* Rookie Read-About Science. Chicago: Children's Press, 1995.

Holmes, Kevin J. *Bees.* Animals. Mankato, Minn.: Bridgestone Books, 1998.

Internet Sites

Bees
http://ezra.mts.jhu.edu/~naomi/insects/bees.html

Bees
http://www.connect.ab.ca/~bautista/insect/bees.htm

Bumblebees: A Flower's Best Friend
http://www.letsfindout.com/subjects/bug/rfibumbe.html

Science World: Exhibits: Bees
http://www.schoolnet.ca/collections/science_world/english/exhibits/bees

Index/Word List

Word Count: 56
Early-Intervention Level: 7

Editorial Credits

Mari C. Schuh, editor; Timothy Halldin, cover designer; Kimberly Danger, photo researcher

Photo Credits

Charles W. Melton, 4
David F. Clobes Stock Photography/Meggy Becker, 20
Dwight R. Kuhn, 10, 12, 14
James Gerholdt, 18
Joe McDonald, cover
Michael Habicht, 16
Rob Curtis, 1, 8
Visuals Unlimited/Bruce Gaylord, 6

Hillsboro
**School
District 1J**
Lenox Elem